# ". . . AND GULLIVER RETURNS"

## --In Search of Utopia--

## Book 2

## WE ARE DIGGING OUR ECOLOGICAL CRYPT?

# "…AND GULLIVER RETURNS"

## In Search of Utopia

## Book 2

## WE ARE DIGGING OUR ECOLOGICAL CRYPT?

By
Lemuel Gulliver XVI as told to Jacqueline Slow

Dear friends—Obviously I wrote this series to be read from Book 1 to the end, but silly me! Readers often begin with what sounds interesting to them. This may leave them unaware of the characters, my friends and I. So let me introduce them. We were boyhood friends, as wild and as close as geese heading south for the winter. But our university educations split us philosophically like a drop of quicksilver hitting the floor. But like those balls of mercury, when brought together, they again become one. As have we.

Ray became a Catholic priest and moved far to the right of where our teenage liberalism had bound us. Ray calls himself a neo-conservative. We think he is a reactionary.

Lee slid to the left of our adolescent leanings, and somewhere along the line became an atheist. Lee is a lawyer.

Concannon, Con for short, retired from his very successful business. I guess his business experience moved him a bit to the right, to conservatism—a conservative just to the right of the middle.

Then there's me. I think I'm pretty much a middle of the roader—except for my passion to save our planet by reducing our population before global warming, massive poverty and far-reaching famines decimate our humanity. Hope this introduction makes our discussions make a bit more sense.

By the way, as most of you know, we have put our photos before every bit of dialogue. This should make you more familiar with us. So the books read more like plays. Since most of you read the books in PDF or EPUB format it is no problem. But if you read them in RTF or TXT you will probably lose the photos. This will make the transitions of the conversations more difficult to follow. LG

**CONTENTS**

-- "Well guys, it's been an entertaining morning. How about letting me buy you lunch. My all time favorite restaurant has been tantalizing my taste buds during all my years in space. You wanna take a drive to Hollywood for lunch at Micelli's?"

-"Don't think I know the place."

- "My dad introduced me. He said that their first place in Hollywood was a pizza parlor where he had his first pizza when he was in high school. They then opened a place on Highland where the décor is an old Italian street. One room has a huge painting of the Grand Canal in Venice. But the best thing is the singing waiters and waitresses. Hollywood is full of talented people waiting to be discovered. Many wait tables, so what is more logical than to let them sing while they work. You get everything from opera to pop. Really fun. How about it?"

—"I've been there. Let's go. But let's keep talking about the issues."

"Forty minutes down the Ventura Freeway, right on the Hollywood Freeway, a quick right and there we are."

-There's Universal City just across Highland. Wonder what new attractions they've got since I was last there? Just park there next to the restaurant.

"Hey Hector, still working here? Guys, Hector was my running back when I coached football at Hollywood High. They were called the Sheiks. The nickname came from Rudolph Valentino's film 'The Sheik.' You remember the late James Garner from the movies? He played end for Hollywood. He played against my dad at LA High. He was then Jim Baumgardner. Carol Burnett went there too. You remember the late John Ritter. He was student body president there. His father was the most popular country western singer of his day, Tex Ritter. But few at the school knew it. John wanted to go it alone. Then there were Lana Turner and Jane Powell, and lots more. They still have a Theater Arts Magnet School within the regular high school. So they're still turning out talent.

"Hector, can we have the table up there next to the Grand Canal?"

-"I feel like I'm sitting at the Doge's Palace. Can almost hear a gondolier singing Santa Lucia. The only thing missing is the stench of the Venetian garbage!"

–"You old romantic, Lee. You'd probably complain about a Papal audience in St. Peter's because it was too dark in the cathedral. One time I was sitting behind the Harlem Globetrotters at a Papal audience. Would you have complained about that?"

—"Not if Goose Tatum showed me his bounce swisher off the marble floor."

–"You blasphemous old rebel. Hope you can play hoops for the Red Devils after you die. Don't think St. Peter will let you into our place. But maybe we can get a home and home between your devils and my angels."

"Great, as long as we don't play in St. Petersburg or Los Angeles, our city of the angels."

–"You probably would want the game in Hell, Michigan or in Hell's Kitchen in New York."

–"You guys never change. You've been cutting each other since junior high school! Want to continue our discussion about the problems of the world? Or do you just want to keep playing one-upmanship? If you do Lee, remember that God's on Ray's side now. If you try your left hook on him now, God will probably smite you. I wouldn't test it!

"Anyway, the major question of the day is how can we get the people of the world, and especially their political, business and religious leaders to overcome their apathy about the problems that overpopulation and technology have saddled us with?"

–"I think we have to look at what Toynbee said, based on his analysis of history 'Apathy can be overcome by enthusiasm, and enthusiasm can only be aroused by two things: first, an ideal, which takes the imagination by storm, and second, by a definite intelligible plan for carrying that ideal into practice.'"

"I've talked a bit about a plan for reducing the population, but maybe we have to look first at developing that imperative ideal that takes the people's imaginations by storm. I think we have to make the people internalize the realities of the threats to our ecology through both our ecological excesses and our ecological scarcities. How do we make them realize that more people means more land cleared of trees for homes and agriculture, more garbage, so more methane and $CO_2$, more power plants for energy production, more cement plants, more natural gas burning and more gasoline burning in trucks, cars and planes—and less water, minerals and food."

## EXCESSES AND SCARCITIES—RECOGNIZING THE PROBLEMS

–"I assume you mean the human caused excesses like air and water pollution, increased warming due to CO2 and other greenhouse gases, and the increase of garbage and other wastes."

–"Right! And scarcities like oil, ocean fish, arable land, potable water and such. Did you know that the federal government has had to cut off water supplies for farming in California—million of acres without water."

–"Don't you think everybody knows about those? My gosh, people have been preaching about raping the planet for at least fifty years."

–"That's true, but most people haven't internalized it. When gasoline prices went over $2 a gallon in the U.S. in 2005, people became upset. But in Europe gasoline prices had been two or three times that level for years and people didn't think anything about it. Then as American gasoline prices advanced, the European prices stayed two to three times higher.

"With more people we will need more homes, so we can use mountains, deserts or farmland. We may build high rises to reduce the amount of land used so we will need more cement, sand and steel. Producing the cement and steel increases the carbon dioxide release and transporting them to the building sites will use energy, probably oil. The sand is becoming more of a problem. Resorts don't want you taking their beaches. As we build on the deserts it is harder to find cheap sand. So building around North Africa isn't so much of a problem since the Sahara is right next door. But it's already hot there and with global warming the air conditioning bills will be astronomical. Los Angeles is really pretty much of a desert. There's still a lot of sand around Palm Springs, but much of it has been covered by rambling ranch houses, resorts and golf courses.

"Then there is the cost of food. With more gullets on the globe, and more gourmets in the kitchen, the people with the 'bread' want more than bread. Rice and wheat are now mere accompaniments to the surf and turf delicacies of fish and steak. Caloric necessities are exceeded with every second helping. From Hong Kong to Paris gourmets' garbage clogs the sewers and landfills. With farmland producing biofuels and supporting housing, agriculture cannot keep up with global glut of empty bellies. So more Third World children starve to death. More middle class Westerners cut back on the necessities which are less important than food. Globalization scatters its rewards and extracts its penalties. And all but the rich must tighten their belts.

–"People have to see the problems now, not tomorrow or in the near future. When sport fishermen can't catch their limits in the ocean they may realize that the oceans have been overfished. When people who love swordfish are warned about eating it because of mercury poisoning, they may be concerned. When their vacations cost more because of fuel cost increases and food prices; when the ozone layer offers less protection against skin cancer so beach vacations are less desirable; when ski areas get less snow because of global warming—vacations will be affected. When taxes are increased to finance cleaning up the environment or to reduce the use of natural resources—it will start to make an effect. Hitting people in the pocketbook tends to get their attention. When energy costs much more, the poorer people won't be able to afford it. The fog of poverty will enshroud a greater number of people. Gasoline and electricity costs will reduce the use of automobiles, air conditioning, heating, dishwashing, clothes washing and drying and many other things both personal and commercial. For all but the richest people, energy will change our lives."

-- "Natural resources are being reduced daily. Just look at corn. With the increased use of corn for biofuels, corn prices go up. So it costs more to feed the livestock, so beef prices rise. What shall we use the corn for? To feed people, to feed cows, to feed cars and trucks? Wheat, rice and other cereal prices have jumped double digits in a day. Increased population increases the need for food. Increased industrialization increases the need for petroleum and other oils. Financial ability controls the destiny of food and oils. And the poorest are left to starve.

"In looking at biofuels the picture is somewhat confusing. While they will reduce the dependence on foreign oil, corn based fuel only reduces the carbon dioxide emissions by 20% while switchgrass generated fuels reduce them by 70%. But methane generated from sewage, manure and organic garbage would kill two birds with one stone, or should we say 'two turds with one groan'-- of your engine.

"But seriously, People think that because the agricultural revolution of the 1970s produced a great deal more food it will continue to function that way. But a recent report from the Chicago Council on Global Affairs states that there will be a 2% reduction in agricultural output per decade because of droughts caused by reduced rainfall in some areas, such as happened in California for a number of years and in other Southwestern states. Higher temperatures are also a factor. They did not even mention the yearly reduction in arable land through windstorms, rain runoff and the building of houses and businesses on what was once farmland. This 2% reduction in agricultural output is magnified in terms of famine outbreaks when we understand that the world population increases by 7 to 8% per decade. This clearly portends much more starvation and many more famines than we have today. Naturally food prices will rise significantly. For years the Department of Agriculture has shown price increases of 3% or more every year. So global warming is going to hit everyone's pocketbook! (1)

"There's more. The estimates are that by about 2030 maize production can be off by 30% in Africa and by 10% in South Asia. In fact India could drop by as much as 40% by the year 2100, while the population in that area is expected to double. So the production in the temperate zones is expected to decrease significantly, as warming increases the temperature in the northern latitudes more farmland will be open in northern Russia, Northern Canada and northern China. But it won't be enough to feed the expected rise in population.

—"Bad metaphor, or is it a simile? I always get them mixed up! But you have probably heard that the there may be a net ecological negative from increasing farmland at the expense of forests and grassland. And if we are trying to feed the poor people in undeveloped lands, using grains for gasoline will reduce their food supply, because hungry mouths are increasing faster than food grains are raised.

"The United Nations relies on its members for contributions to its World Food Program. But with nearly every country's budget in the red, the budget allotment for food for the poor is reduced, and what that money can buy is significantly reduced every year. Will the rich reduce their appetites for food or travel? Never! So the poorest of the poor will starve to death more often. Over ten years ago, in 2008, the United States had to reduce its contribution of food and money. A 40% rise in grain costs minimized what the dollar could buy. And of course, under President Bush, the dollar had lost half of its value. So you had fewer dollars, which were worth less, buying \ that cost more. So the poor in Africa, Latin America, and Asia suffered the consequences.

"And look at China. Its industrialization has been responsible for more than two-thirds of the increased demand for aluminum, zinc and copper. Every year its needs for oil increase by a million gallons of oil per day over what it used the previous year. And India isn't far behind."

—"Certainly some will be concerned about their progeny. But the 'now' is nearly always all-important when compared with concerns about the future. I am proud of the Catholic Church. Pope Benedict, years ago, told Catholic youth to be eco-friendly and to help save the planet. He said we have to safeguard creation. He told the half million youths at Loretto that 'Courageous choices that can re-create a strong alliance between man and earth must be made before it is too late."

—"I'll bet he didn't say anything about controlling the population that is trashing God's planet! I wonder if the pope knows about Father Morris up in Wyandotte, Michigan. I was up in Michigan with my cousin a few years ago. Father Morris put up an electricity generating windmill on his house. Then he had solar panels on the roof and a solar water heating system. His efforts reduced his churches demand for energy by 60% and saved his parish $20,000 a year. He told me that this world is God's creation, 'If someone like me doesn't speak about its care, who will? The changes we've made here are a form of preaching.' But it doesn't stop at his church, he has spread the word to many other churches, and of course, to his parishioners. He said he is just doing as God commanded in Genesis 2:15—we are required to take care of our, our earth."

—"You would think that the knowledge of science would be enough to change people's attitudes and that a real attitude change would result in changed behavior.

"People always fear change. People feared electricity when it was invented, didn't they? People feared coal. They feared gas-powered engines and horseless carriages. There will always be ignorance, and ignorance leads to unwarranted fears. Look at the resistance to computers, to e-mail, to the internet, to mobile phones. Often people resist change because God is against it. Like stem cell research or cloning. Then once people accept it, God seems to accept it too."

—"Is that what is meant in Matthew 16:19 that whatever you shall bind on earth shall be bound in heaven? It makes me wonder why God didn't get it right to start with! Why does He let people tell him what truth will be?"

—"How much more knowledge do we need. It is clear that the human race is living beyond its means. We have created huge problems by depleting our natural resources while increasing excesses that may never be effectively dealt with. We have depleted nature's bounty in many areas. There are far fewer fish in the sea. There is less water in the ground. There is less breathable air. There are fewer natural resources. We are also complicating our lives, and leaving our children with perhaps insurmountable problems relative to global warming because of our man-made greenhouse gasses. The developed nations multiply annually the garbage they must burn or hide in canyons. Their electrical needs often are satisfied with energy produced by fossil fuel burning, with its severe ecological consequences, or by nuclear power generation with its attendant toxic waste that must be hidden. We have polluted our water and our air. Scarcely a human need has not been affected negatively by our selfish need for the good life today. The problem is here and now, forget tomorrow!"

—"As a Republican neo-conservative, I have had to find fault with some of our national leaders. The needs of American business were found to take precedence over the needs of the world in the near and distant future. I was appalled when the Bush administration had proposed laws that would have let many power plants, refineries and factories avoid installing costly new pollution controls to help offset any increased emissions caused by repairs and replacements of their equipment. Energy companies said the two rules the administration proposed in 2002 and 2003 would help them expand energy supplies at lower costs to consumers. But I sided with the environmentalists who said the change would result in just the kind of increased pollution that the law was intended to control. When several states sued the federal government, the court sided with the states."

—"Well Ray you're one of the good reactionaries. I guess God showed you the way that time! But seriously, there were laws passed that called for companies to build plants with modern control technologies, because pollution controls must be modernized along with the plants themselves."

---"You don't get something for nothing. Lower energy costs are the result of simpler more pollution-producing methods. Do you want lower electrical bills and more hurricanes, and flooding and higher food costs because of the higher cost of water and the increased value of farm land due to urbanization, or do you want a cleaner more human friendly atmosphere?"

—"I think all of us here want a cleaner world. Most of the leaders in my party back environmental intelligence. Just look at Arnold Schwarzenegger when he was governor of California, he believed that things needed to happen immediately. I guess that's the difference between a politician who is controlled by business interests and a real leader."

–"But look at the trouble poor Arnold got himself into when he tried to do what was best for the state rather than succumb to the interests of the state employees' unions. That's one of the troubles with modern democracy, the elites are still in control. Business, labor, the military, along with the ensconced political leaders, run the show. They just give the voters enough jellybeans to keep their minds off the pork barrels. It's so rare to have a real leader today in a democracy."

–"Maybe Arnold was just concerned that the melting Arctic and Antarctic ice caps would flood his state. Just think of what a few meters of rising oceans would do to San Diego, Balboa Bay, Los Angeles and

San Francisco. Heck the global warming may submerge California before the big quake topples it into the ocean!"

—"It's no joke, the studies show that by the end of this century the average world temperature can be four degrees higher than today. It's been 130,000 years since that's happened. Oceans can rise 12 to 20 feet higher."

—"No problem. Just wait for the next ice age. During the last one the sea level may have dropped 20 feet. There may actually have been ice ages that dropped the ocean level over 300 feet. Maybe we should buy ocean floor real estate for our descendants! We should be able to drive to Catalina Island. It won't be an island in 10,000 years. Heck maybe we will be able to ski in the Hollywood hills!

"Ray, what did Schwarzenegger plan to do?"

—"He called for reducing the state's greenhouse gas emissions to the 2000 levels by 2010, to the 1990 levels by 2020, and 80 percent below the 1990 levels by 2050. He has also called for hydrogen fueling stations for the eventual hydrogen powered car and for a state subsidy for a million solar roof houses to convert solar power to electricity."

—"All that while he was driving his gas guzzling Humvee?"

—"Didn't you hear? He sold his Humvee and started riding his motorcycle, then he bought an electric car. But back to the issue. I understand that in the past we have had higher temperatures. They certainly weren't caused by industry and cars. And scientists aren't sure why these temperature changes occur."

## PLANETARY TEMPERATURE VARIATIONS—ICE AGES AND WARMING

—"That's true. We've had ice ages and we've had global warming. And only a few degrees up or down from the average temperature can give us an ice age or a period of global warming. The last great ice age ended about 18,000 years ago so we're getting kind of close to the next one."

—"What caused the ice ages?"

—"An ice age requires only a drop of one to 5 degrees Celsius from the Earth's normal temperature of about 15 degrees Celsius. The last major ice age may have been only 3 to 5 degrees Celsius cooler than today, although some estimate it as low as 12 degrees colder

"No one knows why the temperature dropped. Possibly several different actions worked together. Among the theories are the astronomical actions that occur. Here we are talking about the changes in the shape of the Earth's orbit, the variations in the wobble of our planet's axis, and the amount of sunspot activity. Our orbit is not always the same, it changes from a somewhat round orbit to a more elliptical orbit. When it is more elliptical we swing farther from the sun. This change takes about 100,000 years to complete. The wobble in the tilt of the Earth's axis, which may vary almost 2 degrees from its normal 23 degree tilt, allows more sunlight to a different part of the planet. This shift takes about 41,000 years to complete. Then there are the solar eruptions like sun spots. They put out some extra heat but their major effects are magnetic. This strongly affects ultraviolet and x-ray emissions that do affect the upper regions of our atmosphere. The solar activity occurs in two cycles, an 11 year and a 206 year series of cycles.

"Then there are the so-called tectonic causes. By this we mean the shifting of the plates on the outer surface of our planet. Sometimes it is called 'continental drift'. For example what now is Antarctica was once at the equator a half a billion years ago."

– "Does that mean that penguins evolved from parrots?"

–"Maybe. It's just like the movies, we went from black and white to color, and from silent films to the 'talkies!' So it was from parrots to penguins!"

—"You wanna hear more about ice ages or do you want to play Bob Hope and Jerry Seinfeld?"

—"Lets get back to tectonics."

—"Well the shifting of continents can cause changes in the ocean currents which can warm or cool different parts of the world. Ice ages seem to be particularly likely when there is land over the poles.

"There are the oceanic factors, like the Pacific's el Nino and la Nina, that warm or cool the ocean every few years. They also affect rainfall and draughts along with their temperature changes.

"Then there are the atmospheric causes like the accumulation or reduction of greenhouse gases and microscopic particles in the air. So volcanic smoke or smoke from autos or industry can play a part. And water vapor or carbon dioxide and other gases can play a part. That's what the present concern about global warming is about—humans putting more $CO_2$ into the air from burning fossil fuels, more methane from the decomposition of garbage and more other compounds from the products of our technology, such as air conditioning refrigerants and spray cans. The $CO_2$ and methane have always been with us—at least since plants and animals have been a part of our world. We have just increased them excessively. Other gases, like the fluorocarbons, are new to our atmosphere because of our technology. Then there is the possibility that heat from the core of the Earth could come to the surface at various times and create a warming cycle.

"The combination of these can increase the amount of infrared and ultraviolet rays emitted from the sun or absorbed by the land and seas. They can also affect the amount of heat reflected back into space by ice and snow. They reflect about 90% of the light they receive back toward space. If we have less ice we'll have less heat reflected back. On the other hand, the ocean absorbs 90% of the heat that hits it.

"While ice ages are actually the more normal pattern of climate, periods of warming and cooling occur in cycles. This is well understood, as is the fact that small-scale cycles of about 40 years exist within larger-scale cycles of 400 years. These in turn exist inside still larger cycles of 20,000 years, and so on. And for some reason CO2 seems to always be present during warming. The problem today, of course, is the increase in greenhouse gases. Air bubbles from ice cores in Antarctica show that when temperatures rise there is more carbon dioxide in the air. We don't know why. Does the CO2 cause the warming or is it caused by it? Of course in the past it was always from natural causes. But now it is largely from man-made sources.

"About 75 years ago some scientists believed that humans were speeding us towards another ice age because pollutants were blocking out the sunlight. And the world did seem to be cooling then. But in the 1970s temperatures started rising dramatically. For the first time in planetary history humans were changing the climate. With all the factors moving temperatures up and down, there is no question that the trend is upward."

—"Well hasn't the human induced warming today been positive? It helped us out of a mini-ice age. If so maybe it was one of the greatest of human achievements—even though it was not planned. Maybe we should promote the warming to prevent the next ice age?

"After all, ice ages are not all bad. The last ice age gave us the land bridge across the Bering Sea that allowed the Asian migration to populate the Western Hemisphere. Then as the world warmed the land bridge was submerged, cutting migration. As it warmed more, about 8,000 years ago it allowed for agriculture in the world, and as crops became easier to raise we developed crafts, then, trade, then civilization."

—"And don't forget wars, civilization brought disagreements, acquisitiveness, certainty of beliefs, religions—and wars."

—"The last small temperature dip of only about a half of one degree in the mid-1800s is thought to be responsible for such things as the Irish Potato famine. Without that famine we wouldn't have had so many of you dumb Irishmen populating our beautiful country."

—"But without us you wouldn't have had John Kennedy, James Cagney, Ronald Reagan or Wreck and me!"

**GLOBAL WARMING**

—"I've heard that the current global warming actually started during the Industrial Revolution."

—"Right. We can see that from the sediment patterns in Arctic lakes. Warming patterns started in the 1850s. They have just been hugely accelerated during the last few years. And it's going to get worse, much worse. Since the Industrial Revolution it is estimated that between 165 and 290 billion metric tons of carbon dioxide have been added to the atmosphere by industrial nations through the burning of coal, oil, and gas. When I started my voyage the yearly CO2 emissions were almost 25 billion tons a year. That's billion tons, so we're talking about trillions of pounds. And that has increased annually by over a billion tons every year.

"Since the Industrial Revolution the Earth has warmed about 1.4 degrees Fahrenheit. If we don't reduce carbon dioxide emissions to about zero immediately the Earth could warm by 7.2 degrees Fahrenheit by 2100. If we don't get emissions to 0 by 2300 the Earth's temperature will rise 15 degrees Fahrenheit. That's 8 degrees Celsius. (2) And just a 2 degree Celsius rise will cause huge problems for all of us.

"The U.S. and China are the biggest polluters, but on a per capita basis the U.S. is number one while China is 6th in the world."

—"Who else are the leading polluters per person?"

—"Australia is second and Saudi Arabia third. Then Canada is fourth and surprisingly, North Korea is fifth.

"The United Nations Intergovernmental Panel on Climate Change report of 2007 said that cleaning it up will cost less than continuing to pollute. The estimated cost of stabilizing the greenhouse gasses is only about 0.12% of a nation's yearly economy. That is cheap when compared with the cost of rising oceans wiping out huge cities and displacing their populations, fighting the increasing number of forest fires and hurricanes, and the developing shortage of fresh water. Among the benefits would be less sickness due to less air pollution and a stabilization of the rising air temperatures. It will take a long time to reverse what we have done. Nothing but a sharp drop in population will make a relatively quick change.

"From our measurements we know that the level of CO2 during the ice age was 180 parts per million, with the Industrial Revolution it went to about 280 parts per million, but in the last 50 years it has gone over 400 parts per million. Half of these emissions have occurred since the mid-1970s. Methane, another greenhouse gas, increased from 700 parts per million before the Industrial Revolution to 1900 parts per million today. There are also a number of atmospheric gases that were not around a couple of hundred years ago, but modern technology has developed them and released them into the atmosphere at an alarming rate.

"In recent years we've had the Kyoto Accords of the late 1990s and Al Gore's 2006 Academy Award winning documentary that inflamed the concern of many, except for the U.S. president at the time. But climate concerns go back many years earlier. While scientists saw the problems many years earlier, popular magazines were warming up to the subject in the 1960s.(3) As early as 1863 John Tyndall was writing about greenhouse gases and before 1900 the Swedish scientist Svante Arrehenius made the first known attempt to calculate the impact of increased carbon dioxide on the Earth's atmosphere.

"Of the hottest recorded years, 19 of the 20 occurred during the twenty years prior to my trip. There has been a 0.6 degree Celsius increase in temperature in the last century. It seems to be primarily of our own making. The greenhouse effect may also cause extremes of high and low temperatures while the highs will be primary.

"Greenland icecaps have melted more than twice as fast each decade since 1995, the increase was enough to supply about a billion urban city dwellers water for a year—if it could have been captured. If all of Greenland's ice melted it would raise the ocean levels about 23 feet and if the ice in Antarctica melted it would raise the oceans about 200 feet.

"Ice at the poles is categorized as perennial ice and seasonal ice. The perennial ice should remain, but the seasonal ice melts in summer and freezes in winter. The perennial ice contains more air bubbles that scatter the solar light, so less heat is absorbed. But the seasonal ice is more solid and so absorbs more solar energy. It therefore melts faster and warms the ocean more. From 1980 to 2000 the Arctic perennial ice was shrinking at a little less than 1% per year. In 2004 it shrunk 14%.So we lost an amount of ice about equal to the size of Texas.

—"I've heard lower rates of melting, like 6% a year."

—"It depends on how you measure, by coring, taking satellite photos or other means For example, the study you are citing was a NASA satellite study. It showed a 1 ½% loss of ice per decade but a 6% loss in a year in this century. That's a huge increase

"While the scientists are now nearly universally agreed on the reality and the problems of global warming, the politicians may not. While Prince Charles of England said that "if you look at the latest figures on climate change and global warming … they're terrifying, terrifying," President Bush in the U.S.A. didn't see it as much of a problem. The success of American business and getting more and cheaper oil were far more important.

"But the non-business backed IPCC saw it quite differently. The Nobel Peace Prize winning IPCC, formed by the United Nations in 1988 to determine the state of the climate change, has issued four main sets of reports. The first and second reports, in 1990 and 1995, laid the groundwork for the 1997 Kyoto Protocol. The third report, in 2001, and the fourth report released in 2007, were increasingly alarming in warning that we are causing a dramatic alteration of our environment by heating up the atmosphere."

– "I guess as a species we may be lucky if we survive another century or two. Lots of scientists aren't sure we'll survive that long. But there is always hope. We can be like the boxer who is knocked down and is almost out but staggers to his feet because there is a chance that he can win. But as a society we've got to get up now—and fight."

—"OK Rocky, I'm with you. We're down, but not out, yet. So how do we attack the problem? It scares me half to death!"

—"Look out Con, you've been scared half to death, if it happens again you might be all the way dead! But seriously, maybe I haven't been paying enough attention to the causes of the problem and the possible solutions. Can you fill me in quickly, Wreck?"

—"In a nutshell, there is a great deal of carbon in the world. There is also a great deal of oxygen. In the early years of the planet, and until about 150 years ago there was generally enough of a greenhouse effect of the carbon dioxide to allow life to grow and flourish."

—"I thought the 'greenhouse effect' was bad."

—"It is a matter of degree. Keeping out harmful rays of the sun and letting out excess heat is good. But we need more forests to deplete the excess of $CO_2$. The reduction of forests along with the increase of $CO_2$ parallel each other . We need trees and other plants to convert the $CO_2$ back to $O_2$. But too much $CO_2$ along with other so-called greenhouse gases, like methane, create an excessive greenhouse effect—reflecting too much of the Earth's heat back to the planet's surface rather than letting it go back into space.. That's where we are now. Too much heat is being trapped. At the same time some of these greenhouse aerosols have depleted the ozone layer which lets in more harmful rays and increases cancers of the skin."

—"So it's not only increasing our air conditioning bills but it's changing our ecology significantly. So the hotter it gets the more air conditioning we use so the more fossil fuels we burn to produce the electricity for them. So more $CO_2$, so more heat, so more air conditioning needed. What a self-perpetuating cycle!"

—"It's more than just increasing your air conditioning bills! Glaciers are melting faster. The warmth in the northern hemisphere makes the flowers bloom earlier and is increasing the tree growth somewhat. But trees in the temperate zones of California, Europe and Australia are dying more often from parasitic diseases. Warm water parasites are moving northward poisoning the shellfish and ocean fish. These are then killing seals and sea lions."

---"How are they being killed?"

---The red tide, or the phytoplankton, clog the gills of fish so they suffocate. They get into the bodies of shellfish as they feed and poison them. And some algae produce domoic acid, which in low doses can cause miscarriages and brain tissue decay and in high doses is fatal. Fish and shellfish concentrate these toxins then humans and other mammals eat them. Hundreds of California sea lions have died from these poisons. It is affecting fish up the West Coast even north into Canadian waters. Anchovies, salmon, mussels and squid are some of the sea creatures affected. While they are killing sea mammals now, we humans may be next.

"You guys remember how, when the red tide was in, we'd go down to Playa del Rey at night and watch the waves break in a bright florescent blue. Then we'd run along the sand near the water and our feet would kick up that phosphor and it looked like blue flames coming from our feet."

—"I remember. The ocean was beautiful at night but ugly brown in the daylight. And it smelled terrible!"

—"Oh the good old days! But now more on the bad days ahead. Our global warming of the water can also increase the risk of cholera outbreaks thousands of miles away.

—"Then there's the garbage in the oceans. I've heard that sea birds are dying from eating plastic things that have found their way to the seas. As a diver, I've been concerned about the huge increase of diseases in coral due to pollution. It seems to be from the sugars from sewage dumping and agricultural run-off. The increased algae seems to be the problem here too. Fish used to help us by eating algae, but the overfishing has reduced that protection.

"I used to dive in the Caribbean but the dumping of live sewage into the water made it less appealing and the reefs were disappearing because of the sewage. Too many people and not enough sewage treatment plants. I gave up surfing in California because of the danger of hepatitis. It's hard to believe that just driving my car and heating my house has such wide ranging effects for my quality of life."

--"Insufficient oxygen, or hyperoxia, in the oceans is causing three times more males to be born in some species of fish and shrimp—and the females born have twice the amount of testosterone as normal. Then there are 100,000 square miles of oxygen-dead zones in the ocean as farm run off, such as fertilizer kill the sea life. (4) So our problems are not only caused by carbon dioxide."

-":It's strange to understand that the carbon and oxygen from things living millions of years ago is causing our problems today? When dinosaurs died they took their carbon with them to the grave. When trees, mosses, grasses and marine life died, their carbon was buried with them. Then 'abra cadabra' we have oil and coal."

—"Seriously, carbon is one of the most prevalent elements in the world. Scientists know of about ten million carbon compounds, from the super tough diamond and our necessary vitamins to gases like carbon monoxide and carbon dioxide. What we are doing is taking carbon based fuel, that took a million years of life to produce, then using it driving to the market or in heating our houses for a day. So we are well past the level of carbon dioxide that allowed life to develop and flourish. We are now choking on a level of the gas that life cannot tolerate. It's like other things, there is a right amount and there is an excessive amount."

–"Like vitamin A, you need some, but too much in a short period of time can be lethal."

—"Or eating fats. You need some for normal body functioning, but too much and you become obese or die from a cancer or a heart problem."

–"So while some of the excess carbon dioxide may be absorbed in the oceans, they can't absorb it all. So the world warms. This increases draught and forest fires which release more $CO_2$ into the air because of the carbon that was retained by the trees when they took in the carbon dioxide from the air and gave off oxygen for animals to breathe. The process of photosynthesis, which we all know about, requires that the trees and plants retain the carbon they took from the air. Also, as the world warms, plant life which was frozen in the northern hemisphere's tundra in Russia and North America thaws and $CO_2$ is released. So while it was the human activities of heating, driving and manufacturing that started the warming ball rolling, that spark has ignited additional carbon releasing processes. It's like starting to drive down a steep hill. You provide the gas to get your car rolling down, but even if you shut off the engine you will be going faster and faster. It's that snowball effect. We've started it, but we can't stop it."

—"Where will this extra carbon come from?"

—"Some of the computer models show it coming primarily from the oceans, others show it coming from the land. I think it is more likely to come from the land. Studies from England show that the land is giving up 14 million tons of carbon a year. Then as warming increases more carbon is released. Then we add in the reduced carbon dioxide uptake from South American rainforests because of a lack of rain and we add to the problem."

—"Is it really that dire, Wreck?"

–"It is. But we can slow the process. But reversing it, so that the greenhouse gasses are reduced enough to cool the planet, is highly improbable right now, in spite of the attention that most scientists and concerned citizens, like Al Gore, have brought to the problem. The world's citizens bury their heads in sands of hope, but as with the proverbial ostrich, the problem still exists, whether they can see it or not.

"None of the immediate solutions are palatable. A nuclear holocaust wiping out over five billion people would solve one problem, but the nuclear radiation and fallout would just substitute one problem for another. Germ warfare or poisons could have the same outcomes.

"A quick reduction of population would work, but population cannot be reduced quickly peacefully. Another solution could be to require immediate drops in fossil fuels for driving and manufacturing. We could reduce fossil fuel use ten percent per year, and allow only clean energy to make up the difference. This would force government, businesses and the populations to bear the brunt of the prevention of the genocide of the planet's human population –a genocide not anticipated by the originators of the Industrial Revolution and the race to riches that they created.

"In spite of the dire warnings that should disturb us all and change our path toward self destruction, we continually increase our production of greenhouse gasses. At the present rate of continually increasing our $CO_2$ production, the amount held in the atmosphere will double in this century. (5) At the same time, the Earth's ability to absorb the $CO_2$ is being reduced as forests disappear to make room for housing and to provide the lumber for that housing.

"An immediate and sharp reduction in population is necessary. We should be planting billions of trees. And of course we would need to use only non-polluting sources of energy, like: wind, geothermal, tidal, hydrogen and solar. We'd have to find ways of handling the garbage so that we don't create more methane and $CO_2$."

 –"Can't we use methane for cars?"

 —"Of course. And some people have done it for years. The problem would be to trap the escaping gas from the garbage before it reached the atmosphere. Utilizing it is already practical."

—"I've been concerned for years, but when I heard about the computer projections done at the Lawrence Livermore Laboratory a few years ago I really got scared. Have you heard about it Commander, er, I mean, Wreck?"

—"No what did they predict?"

—"Using the facts that you had just alluded to, they projected what will happen in the next two centuries. They predict that the polar areas will increase their temperatures about 68 degrees and the average world temperature will go up almost 15 degrees. And they said that their estimates were conservative, so it could be much worse.

"Every year the carbon dioxide gets a bit worse. From close to 400 parts per million now it should reach 1000 parts per million by early in the next century. Then by the beginning of the 24th century, if we survive that long, it should be nearly 1500 parts per million so we're talking about a 400% increase over today's levels and 800% over the pre-Industrial Revolution levels. Even at the 1000 parts per million level we will have real problems.

"As the frozen tundra thaws, trees should start to grow in those areas so they would capture some carbon. But the tropical areas might get too hot to support the forests, such as those in Brazil."

 --"But plant growth is dependent on soil nutrients."

–"That shouldn't be a problem in the thawed tundra because of all the decayed vegetation in the land. The problem is more in the populated areas where people plant trees, which is good, but they must fertilize them, and they usually do it with petrochemicals."

—"Is carbon dioxide the only problem?"

—"No. There are also methane, nitrous oxide and water vapor that allow the sunlight in but stop the radiated heat from the Earth from escaping back to space so they effectively warm the globe more than would be ideal."

—"Aren't these the same air pollutants we've been talking about since the 1970s?"

—"Some are and some aren't. Since the 70s we have talked about pollutants near the Earth's surface and their effects on our breathing and blood. Now we are more concerned with pollutants miles up in the atmosphere. Sulfur is a problem whether it is high or low. Carbon monoxide is a problem when we breathe it, but when it becomes carbon dioxide it is a problem high up. Ozone is a toxic compound for plants and animals at ground level, but at high altitudes it is a positive factor since it filters out some of the sun's harmful ultraviolet rays. Lead is a problem at low levels but isn't a factor high in the atmosphere. Some of the aerosols are inert at ground level but may break down the ozone layer when they rise to the stratosphere. Carbon dioxide isn't much of a factor at ground level but is a major negative factor in global warming when it rises several miles above the earth. So you see there are huge differences in what chemical compounds may do at the higher and lower altitudes.

## GREENHOUSE GASES THE CAUSES OF INCREASED WARMING

"Let's start with the ultimate cause of warming—the sun. Our energy comes from the sun where 700 million tons of hydrogen are converted to energy every second. Only a very small portion of that energy hits the Earth. That energy comes as visible light, which includes the light waves that make up the rainbow, but most of it comes in wavelengths longer than the visible red light, the infrared waves, and wavelengths shorter than the violet waves, the ultraviolet. When you sit in the sun you are warmed mainly by the infrared waves and tanned by the ultraviolet waves.

"About half of the solar energy actually penetrates the Earth's surface of land and sea. The other half was either absorbed by some of the greenhouse gases or clouds or was reflected back to the atmosphere. Snow and ice are good reflectors of this energy, as are clouds, atmospheric aerosols, sand, rooftops, and even the white foam of ocean surf. This is primarily infrared radiation. If there were no greenhouse gases this reflected infrared energy would all go back into space. Some of this is solar energy and heat which was reflected from the Earth is then reflected back to the Earth by the greenhouse gases. This causes global warming. Some of this warming was essential to the development of life. Too much can destroy our ecology and our life.

## THE CASE FOR TODAY'S GLOBAL WARMING REALITY

"We can get a picture of previous cooling and warming periods several ways. By coring through the ice in Antarctica going 2000 feet deep we have been able to sample air as far back as 160,000 years ago. Other drilling in the Atlantic takes us back about three million years. So we have a fair picture of the past temperatures of the Earth. As far as we can see from the air trapped in the ice we can see that CO2 seems to increase when the world is warmer. But we don't know if is it is the cause or the effect?

"We can also see the effects of weather on fossils much older than the 3 million years and we can get a more recent picture by looking at tree rings. Of course now we have weather stations around the world and we get continual satellite readings."

–"I've heard that there is a variation between the satellite readings and the surface temperature readings and that the satellites don't show the same warming patterns."

–"That's true. Temperatures very high up are often lower and can change the temperature readings that the satellite is picking up from the ground. But we are concerned with surface temperature. It's on the surface of the globe that the ice caps are melting and trees in the temperate latitudes are dying. And the warming changes are happening a hundred times faster than anything we have seen in the last three million years of periodic natural warming cycles.

## WATER VAPOR

"Today's problems we attribute to the human caused increase in greenhouse gases. I have to mention that without greenhouse gasses we would not be here. Our average earthly temperatures would be much colder—about 34 degrees Celsius colder. You may not know that water vapor is the major greenhouse gas. It causes about 35 to 70% of the greenhouse effect."

—"36 to 70%, that's a pretty big range. Can't they bring it down to one number or a smaller range?"

—"Well the amount of a greenhouse gas varies somewhat in different parts of the Earth's atmospheric layers. When I give you ranges, like 36 to 70% the higher number is more appropriate for the gas alone, but since none are found alone and the percentages of the various gases vary with altitude and with its location over the land and sea masses the effects of a particular gas can be lower than its maximal heat reflecting level. .

"A major factor in the amount of water vapor in the air is the air temperature. At 40 degrees Celsius the warm air can hold 5 grams of water per 100 grams of dry air. At 30 degrees 100 grams of dry air can hold about 3 grams of water, at 20 degrees 1.5 grams of water vapor, at 10 degrees—about a half a gram and at freezing—about 4/10s of a gram. The higher the altitude or the closer to the poles, the colder it gets.

"Since the area near the equator is warmer we find more water vapor in the air. This creates the major storms like we've seen in Bangladesh and the Caribbean. Because the warm air can evaporate surface water it contributes to the drying of lakes and seas like Lake Chad in Africa, the Aral Sea in Asia and the Sea of Galilee in the Middle East.

"We live in the troposphere, the lowest level of our atmosphere. It is about 4 miles high at the poles and 12 miles at the equator. Above that is the stratosphere. Most water vapor and about 80% of the other greenhouse gases are in the troposphere. The ozone layer is in the stratosphere, up to about 10 to 20 miles."

—"I've heard that $CO_2$ is only about 3% or less of the greenhouse gases."

—"That's true. Water vapor accounts for about 95% of greenhouse gases and causes about 50% of the global warming. As I said, the estimates vary from 35 to 70% of the warming. Of the rest, $CO_2$ is by far the major one. The 3% content in the atmosphere is responsible for about 15% of the warming. The estimates run from 10 to 25%. And it is the one that seems to be linked to the previous warming and cooling periods in our world.

"Water vapor is not increased by humans except where high levels of evaporation might take place, such as over irrigated fields. However, as the human generated $CO_2$ increases the air temperature, more water vapor can be held by the warmer air, thus increasing the greenhouse effect. This higher humidity is a factor in the increasing strength of tropical storms."

## CARBON DIOXIDE

—"If it weren't for $CO_2$ we wouldn't be around. But where did it come from originally?"

—"It first came out of the Earth's crust and made the atmosphere hospitable to early life. Then it continued spewing and plant life captured it then released it when it decomposed. It helped to stabilize the world's temperature somewhat so animals could develop and evolve. A lot of carbon has been deposited over the last few billion years. Much of it has accumulated as oil and coal were made from life that had died and settled into the bowels of the Earth billions or millions of years ago. Now as we burn the coal and oil we are putting the carbon accumulation of millions of years back into the atmosphere in just a few years.

"Eight hundred billion tons of carbon are dissolved in the world's oceans and in marine plants and animals. Sea shells and coral have been good storage sites for carbon. But as the oceans warm the water can't hold as much carbon dioxide. When the oceans and vegetation can't store it, it accumulates in the atmosphere. The atmosphere holds about 750 billion tons of carbon. We are now putting about 7 billion tons of $CO_2$ into the air every year. As I mentioned, the $CO_2$ accounts for 10 to 25% of the greenhouse effect."

—"Does it all come from oil and coal?"

—"Globally, liquid and solid fuels accounted for over 75% of the emissions from fossil-fuel burning. Combustion of gas fuels, such as natural gas, contributes almost 20% of the CO2.Cement production adds another 3 ½%"

—"Is it primarily our cars and trucks that are doing the damage?"

—"No, CO2 released when we use fossil fuels to power our electricity generating plants cause nearly 40% of the U.S. emissions. Coal accounts for 80 to 90% of that. A problem with coal is that it releases about 80% more carbon than natural gas does per kilowatt produced. Oil ranks about halfway between coal and gas as a pollutant.

"You mentioned cars. Around 20% of CO2 comes from cars and small trucks. For every gallon of gas you use your car engine produces almost 20 pounds of carbon monoxide, about a pound for every mile driven. Since the U.S. uses over 20 million barrels of oil per day, just increasing the average car's gas mileage by 3 miles per gallon would save a million barrels a day. This would save U.S. drivers 25 billion dollars a year. On the other hand, sitting in traffic costs both money and pollutants. One year of gridlock costs about $63 billion for the 2.3 billion gallons of gasoline wasted and it uses millions of hours of drivers' time.

"Another way to look at it is to compare the average American driving the family car 10,000 miles. If it gets 25 miles per gallon the pollutants it produces would equal a year's worth of heating the owner's house by natural gas. If the house were heated with electricity produced by burning coal, driving the car a year would equal the pollutants produced in just four months of coal generated home heating."

—"How do various countries rank, per capita, in terms of CO2 output?"

—"The U.S.A. and China produce more CO2 than any other country—about 6 billion tons a year each. but China has more than three times as many people. Maybe we should look at it from a per capita output. When we do that we find that Qatar heads the list with 70 metric tons per person. The smaller Arab Mideast states are also high, in the 20 plus metric ton range. But the US is right up there at over 20 metric tons per person. Canada is pretty high too, at about 19. Most of the European countries are in the 6 to 15 metric ton range. Mexico averages 4 tons per person which is the world average. Naturally the undeveloped countries range down to 0.

"Since the Industrial Revolution CO2 has increased over 30%. It is not only the major man-made greenhouse gas, it is the longest lasting. While methane in the atmosphere lasts 10 to 12 years, carbon dioxide can last hundreds of years in the atmosphere, and the amount we have already put into the sky may take tens of thousands of years to dissipate, assuming we stopped our CO2 pollution now."

—"How can we get rid of it? I've heard so much about half-life estimates. I've seen estimates for the half life of carbon dioxide of from a couple of years to a hundred years. And it seems that 38 years is the most common number given."

—"You're right. But it depends on such things as the number of trees and other plants in the world and how much more $CO_2$ the ocean can absorb. It has been absorbing about half of the human produced $CO_2$ up to now. But as the ocean warms the $CO_2$ is held closer to the surface and the amount of gas that can be absorbed by the whole ocean is reduced.

"Then there is the fact that when the climate warms, the plants don't absorb as much carbon dioxide, probably because they reduce their growing rate so that they can conserve water. So $CO_2$ emissions are not being handled as well as they were a hundred years ago. But there's more to the mix. As the world warms there is some evidence that the tree line is rising in the northern latitudes and in the higher altitudes. But then there are some other negatives like tree damaging insects that increase as the climate warms. The average temperature is expected to increase by almost one and a half degrees Celsius by 2050. It may not sound like much but on a global scale it is immense. If we do nothing, the Earth's temperature will probably rise 4 degrees Celsius this century."

—"How are all these predictions made?"

—"Predictions of climate change come from several sources. There are the measured temperature record, satellite photos of healthy green vegetation versus brown draught areas, coring into ocean sediment or ice, and computer models where these and other variables are analyzed. While all the predictions are dire, they vary in their catastrophic forecasts because of differences in the computer models used and the information analyzed.

"For example, the estimates for $CO_2$ increases by the end of this century range from 20 parts per million to 200 parts per million. These would increase temperatures from 0.1 degree to 1.5 degrees Celsius. If we average the predictions we will have about a three quarter of a degree Celsius increase.

"In the economic realm the estimates of economic costs of every ton of carbon dioxide that goes into the atmosphere or the oceans average $12 a ton, but the range of predictions is from $3 to $95 a ton. We know it's bad, but we don't know how bad.

"Another area of economic estimates indicate that to stem the dangers of $CO_2$ it would take 1% of the gross domestic product to be invested in reducing carbon dioxide emissions, and if they are not sufficiently reduced a global recession of up to 20% of the world's gross domestic product will occur."

## CARBOM MONOXIDE (CO) TO CARBON DIOXIDE ($CO_2$)

"Of course carbon monoxide is a byproduct of anything that is burned that contains carbon. That includes about every kind of combustion from candles and home fireplaces to cars and rockets. It's a deadly poison, which is why people often commit suicide by running the car in a locked garage and breathing in the fumes. Your red blood cells prefer carbon monoxide to oxygen, but your tissues need oxygen, and the oxygen in the carbon monoxide cannot be released into the blood.. So if there is carbon monoxide in the air your blood cells latch on to it and your blood becomes oxygen starved. At 50 to 70 parts per million you can begin being poisoned and at two or three times that level you will probably be on your way to meeting your Maker.

"In the atmosphere carbon monoxide will eventually combine with oxygen and become carbon dioxide. So whether you are burning wood in a fireplace or candles on your dinner table, you are contributing carbon monoxide and carbon dioxide to our atmosphere."

—"What about methane?"

## METHANE

—"After carbon dioxide, the most significant greenhouse gas is methane. It accounts for 4 to 9% of the greenhouse effect. Its major source is natural gas fields because natural gas is 97% methane. When it is burned we produce more $CO_2$. About 10% of methane comes from biomass burning. Methane is also derived from things like rice paddies, bovine flatulence, bacteria in bogs and from fossil fuel production. Most of the world's rice, and all of the rice in the United States, is grown on flooded fields. When fields are flooded, anaerobic conditions develop and the organic matter in the soil decomposes, releasing methane, $CH_4$, into the atmosphere.

"Although methane is about 200 times less abundant than carbon dioxide in the atmosphere, molecule for molecule methane is 25 times more effective at trapping heat. It has a half life of about ten years in the atmosphere. Since the beginning of the Industrial Revolution, methane has more than doubled in the troposphere. Additionally, its concentration has been increasing about 1% per year.

"As the oceans warm we can expect methane, which has been trapped in the ice under the oceans sediment, to be released. It is estimated that there are ten trillions of tons which could be released. If they were all released at once we might expect another 5 degree increase in global temperature. More likely is the release of methane from the peat bogs of the world where about 70 billion tons are stored.

## OZONE

Ozone is a relatively unstable molecule of three oxygen atoms. At ground level it is an air pollutant that is toxic to the respiratory system. At high altitudes, 15 to 30 kilometers, it acts as a filter of harmful ultraviolet rays, reducing the number that reach the earth. But it also acts as a greenhouse gas trapping infrared rays reflected from the Earth. It accounts for 3 to 7% of the greenhouse effect.

## NITROUS OXIDE

"Then there's nitrous oxide, $N_2O$. You may have heard of the anesthetic called 'laughing gas', that's nitrous oxide. Nitrous oxide is naturally produced by oceans and rainforests. Man-made sources of nitrous oxide include nylon and nitric acid production, the use of fertilizers in agriculture, cars with catalytic converters and the burning of organic matter. Nitrous oxide is broken down in the atmosphere by chemical reactions that involve sunlight. Its concentrations have been increasing at about 0.3 percent per year for the last several decades. Yet, nitrous oxide has a lifetime of 150 years in the atmosphere, which contrasts sharply with the 10-year lifetime of methane. A single nitrous oxide molecule is the equivalent of 200 to 300 carbon dioxide molecules in terms of its greenhouse gas effect. Biomass burning accounts for about 2 to 3 percent of the total amount of troposphere nitrous oxide.

"Emissions of nitrous oxides and methane are further associated with the production of tropospheric ozone. Unlike "good" ozone in the stratosphere that acts as a shield to screen out the sun's harmful ultraviolet rays, ozone in the troposphere is a pollutant that, when breathed, damages lung tissue and is also harmful to plants.

## SULPHUR DIOXIDE

"Acid rain is a major effect of excessive oxides of sulfur. Well over a third of China has been dampened by acid rain from the 25 million tons of sulfur dioxide emitted from their coal and oil burning factories. The Chinese output of sulfur dioxides is increasing almost 10% per year. While the cheaper energy sources are good for business they harm the soil and vegetation. It's not a greenhouse gas but it is certainly an air pollutant.

## INDUSTRIAL SOURCES OF GREENHOUSE GASES

### ELECTRICITY GENERATION

"Let's look at the major pollution cause, power generation.

"On average, about 1400 pounds of $CO_2$ is created for every million kilowatts of electricity produced. Of course it varies from source to source. The different types of coal, oil, water power, wind, natural gas all have quite different polluting effects. Only about 1 to 2% of electricity in the U.S. and the world is generated by renewable sources such as wind, solar, geothermal and tidal power.

"Water power generates only about 6% of the world and US electrical power. Water power generation is, of course, subject to how much rain a watershed gets—and that can vary from year to year. Throughout the world coal, oil and gas provide most of the power for the generation of electricity. They, of course, are the great polluters. With China building nearly 600 coal burning power stations we can expect things to get worse. Although there have been some proposals for building cleaner power plants they would be quite expensive.

### COAL

"The quality of coal is determined by its carbon content. High quality anthracite coal is about 95% carbon and yields about 12,000 British thermal units per pound. Lower grade coals generally contain more than 55% carbon and yield about 7,000 BTUs per pound. In the USA about a billion tons of coal are used every year to produce about half of the country's electricity needs. But of the total power generated, coal is responsible for 80% of the $CO_2$ formed. With every American using over 12,000 kilowatt hours of electricity each day, that's 4 ½ million kilowatts a year, so you can see the problems. The average American uses about 2 ½ times the energy that the average European uses and ten times what the average Central or South American uses. The American also uses 20 times what the typical Far Eastern person uses and 40 times what the African uses. No wonder the US produces so much $CO_2$.

"There's another source. As I mentioned, much carbon is trapped by nature under the permafrost in Russia and Canada. Decayed, but frozen, trees and other vegetation are releasing their stored $CO_2$. Estimates are that 200 to 800 billion tons of carbon would be released to the atmosphere if the permafrost thaws. So we have a doubly negative effect of our fuel burning. Human yearly output of carbon is 'only' about 7 billion tons of carbon—and look at the mess that has gotten us into. Our increased carbon dioxide in the air warms it so that frozen life becomes thawed and releases its carbon. This in turn increases the warming even more."

 —"Are we working towards a solution?"

–"Right now there are more roadblocks than solutions. While any legislator who is not illiterate knows about the global warming problem, they are afraid to address our population increase and its negative effects. But as political pragmatists they seek to make life easier for the electorate. Otherwise they won't get re-elected.

"You may have noticed that there is traffic on the roads. Gridlock is the curse of the car. So the U.S. government plans to spend about $48 billion dollars a year on highways."

–"That will reduce gridlock costs, but it won't if it increases car buying and gasoline usage? And it's not enough money to really solve the problems of traffic for 300 million Americans each driving their own car, alone. I read that they would have to spend $70 billion a year to solve the major problems with traffic. After all, the number of vehicle miles traveled has increased by 100% in the last 30 years, but roads have only increased about 10%."

—"Don't forget commercial trucks that produce about 13% of the $CO_2$ and they need more roads. Then airplanes add another 4% and that increases yearly.

"It's obvious to all that there is too much traffic on the roads. To stop it we must stop people from living modern lives. Would we use our cars if public transportation got us there faster, more comfortably, safer and cheaper? And we should certainly plant more trees."

## EFFECTS OF WARMING

—"What effects will global warming have on our lives?"

--"The ramifications of global warming are vast. Many species will disappear."

—"That may not be so bad as long as it is flies and mosquitoes, and maybe rattlers, but I hope its not pandas and porpoises."

—"You old softy Ray. And don't worry, your teddy bear will ride out the storm! But seriously, there will be huge economic effects. Insurance premiums will rise because there will be more forest fires and more hurricanes. The risk of natural disasters has more than tripled in the last fifty years. Over a third of these have been climate related. The $15 billion a year increase in insurance payouts has to be covered by increased premiums for fire and flood insurance. More deaths occur during heat spells. This will affect heath insurance premiums. National security will be affected because people will be forced to migrate from parched lands and eventually from submerged lands.

"You've heard about what it can do to sea levels. But the evidence is conflicting. 18,000 years ago, at the peak of the ice age, the sea level was 120 meters lower than it is today. For the last 3,000 years the ocean has raised only a foot or two, that's less than a half inch per 100 years. But the predictions now are that warming will increase the sea level over a meter this century. That's more than 3 feet. But, and it's a big 'but', three million years ago when the temperature rose 2 to 3 degrees above today's temperature, the sea level rose by 80 feet, not 3 feet. The ice sheets at that time melted much faster when the temperature changed than we have been predicting today. And you know that the rise in the oceans is caused by both the melting of glaciers and ice sheets that are over land, and the increased volume of the ocean due to its warming. But ice already in the  , like ice burgs, don't change the water level when they melt.

"Some of the effects will depend on where you live. Oceans will rise so coastal living will be destroyed. In less than a hundred years the seas could rise 20 feet, but the projections now are for only a couple of feet. But even this could wipe out costal living from Bangladesh to Malibu. Venice, Italy already has severe problems. And the Netherlands will have to build their dikes much higher, but it's doubtful that the country can survive without periscopes. They'll have to raise seaweed rather than tulips, and cod rather than cows.

"People in hurricane zones will have more and stronger storms. People inland from warmer oceans can expect more tornadoes and much more rain and flooding, such as we have seen in China, Pakistan, India and Europe. People in north and east Africa and southern Europe can expect less rainfall and hotter temperatures, so their agricultural output will drop. In Africa this will lead to more famines. Africa's population, growing at about 7% a year, will be hard hit by droughts. Warming and the lack of water will force migration north. And if the will of Allah or God decrees, northern hemisphere countries will allow for immigration. But the immigrants will bring with them their traditions of family fecundity and the white nations will grey as they continue their socialistic support of siring. We need only look at Darfur to see the conflict caused by the desertification of large areas causing migration. We already have increasing numbers of global warming refugees to add to those fleeing violence. Then there will be the reduction in income from tourism around the Mediterranean because of too much heat and too little water."

—"But there are some positives. The Northwest Passage will open up and reduce the shipping costs and the CO2 emissions from ships going between Europe and Asia. The supertankers that now must travel south of South America, because they are too big for the Panama Canal, will save huge amounts of money in fuel and will be able to make more trips during the summer months. Russia may also gain as Siberia warms. It may open vast areas for agriculture. But then the planet will lose as the Siberian peat bogs release the carbon that they have sequestered since the last ice age.

"But we could replace the energy of all the world's power plants if we could just use effective solar collectors in a small area of the Sahara. An area the size of Portugal would do it.

## HIGHER OCEANS AND MORE ACIDIC OCEANS

"A while ago you mentioned Malibu. Why is it in danger?"

—"Satellite surveys show that arctic ice is melting faster than we thought it would. Snowfall will increase in the polar areas but not enough to make up for the loss of ice through the warming of the air and sea. The biggest ice losses will be from Antarctica. Along with more water, the CO2 absorbed in the water has made the surface water 30% more acidic than it was in the pre-industrial age.

"Acids, like the weak carbonic acid, H2CO3, comes from water vapor and CO2, nitric acid comes from the nitrogen compounds and the strong sulfuric acid H2SO4 is formed by water and sulfur oxides. The sulfur comes primarily from coal burning. The absorption of the greenhouse gases by the ocean reduces the amount of global warming at a cost of increased acidity. But the oceans should be a bit alkaline. The acidity is reducing the ocean animals' abilities to form shells and coral reefs."

"Then there's the flooding problem. The Union for Concerned Scientists, looked at 52 National Oceanic and Atmospheric Administration tide gauges in coastal cities in Florida, Maryland, Georgia, Virginia and other states. The UCS analyzed the states' flooding risk under mid-range sea level rise predictions taken from the White House's National Climate Assessment — an estimate of 5 inches of sea level rise by 2030, and 11 inches by 2045. It found that tidal flooding could triple in some cities in 15 years and occur 10 times as often in most cities in the next 30 years.

"These are not the type of flooding that kills people, but rather the type that does damage to homes and businesses. A rise of the 11 inches in the water level by 2045 would increase the high tide by that much. To tell you what this means, if there was a slope of 1 foot per 30 feet of beach, the high tide would reach 30 feet farther in 2045 than it does today. Then combine that with any higher than normal waves and you have a problem. Then of course if the waves are much higher because of the storms that global warming often increases, you have a multiple problem.

"This doesn't even consider the worst case scenario, which has only a 5% chance of happening—that would be a rise of 6 feet in the sea level by 2100."

-- I always get mixed up with the size of the waves and how high the tide is. Can you clarify that for me a little bit Wreck?

-- Learning about tides was one the first things they taught us when I was a rookie lifeguard for LA County. You know that the sun and the moon pull on the oceans. The moon is more important. As the moon circles around the earth it pulls the water towards it. The water nearest the moon and on the other side of the earth will be in high tides, so we can say that if the moon is at 0° and the other side of the earth is 180°, the water at 90° and 270° would be lower-- so low tide. When I was working at Venice Beach we always had tide books, the same as the fishermen use, to predict the tides. These books tell us to the minute exactly how high the tide would be. In mid-July we had the highest tides of the year, about 7.2 feet above the mean. If we happened to get big surf at the same time, as sometimes happened, we often got water all the way to the back of the beach in pools and several times the door of my lifeguard tower was beaten in by the surf. Sometimes I had to wade to my tower through the 2 foot deep pools created when the big surf crashed over the birm and flowed deep into the beach. So in answer to your question, the tide just tells how high the water level will be then the size of the waves will indicate how much damage will be felt. Both high waves and a high tide can bring water well past what is normal.

"The study I was mentioning showed that the water level in Atlantic City had risen 8 inches. They expect another 11 inches by 2045. This would be about a foot and a half higher water level than 75 years ago. Around here just look at what that could do to Balboa Island. Or look at the beachfront houses south of Washington Boulevard. And look at the damage that water could do to those multi-million dollar movie star houses on the beach at Malibu.

"Look at how many cities are built right next to the ocean: Norfolk, Boston, Charleston, Miami, San Francisco, Seattle, Baltimore. It has already had a significant impact on the coastal cities of China. Naturally the Netherlands is in real trouble—as is Venice, Italy.

-- " I understood that the sea level is rising only 3.2millimeters a year. That would be about 9 inches over the 70 years from 1970 to 2045. That's only about half of what your information says. (6)

-- You have been reading the National Oceanic and Atmospheric Administration's report. I'm proud of you Ray. The NOAA is one of the government's best agencies for reporting the effects of climate change. If you have been reading that you also have read that atmospheric $CO_2$ concentrations are now 395.3 ppm and sometimes exceed 400 parts per million. Last year was one of the warmest on record, ranking between second and sixth, depending on which data sets you use. And the Arctic sea ice have been at their lowest points in each of the last seven years. As a reactionary, I think you're coming into the 21st century rapidly. Congratulations!"

—"I guess I can't get it through my thick head about why warming the water is so bad. It's certainly more comfortable when we go swimming at Zuma."

—" Simply stated, warmer water gives up more water vapor through the evaporation. Warmer air holds more water vapor. So the ocean is giving back warmth by adding water vapor even though it has absorbed much of the heat caused by the greenhouse gases, including the water vapor. But then there is another thing happening. When the water absorbs carbon dioxide it creates an acid, carbonic acid."

—"I remember that from chem class. Water, H2O, plus carbon dioxide, CO2, forms carbonic acid, $H_2CO_3$.

—"Right you are. You probably make the old Notre Dame football coach and chemistry teacher, Knute Rockne, smile in his hallowed grave."

—"You don't know how hallowed that grave is until you have lived through a Notre Dame football season! But what problems might the acidification of the oceans cause?"

--"Shellfish, squid and many of the lower animals are greatly affected. Shellfish cannot make their shells if the ocean is too acid. This also affects reefs and the formation. At the current level fish are not generally affected by their eggs may well be. Also as the lower-level animals like brittle stars are reduced there is less food for sea mammals like seals. So by affecting lower level sea life, the food chain can be disrupted severely.

"When you understand that almost 94% of the warming has gone into the oceans you can see how it can affect our seas and sea life. So far only about 2.4% percent has gone into the atmosphere. That has warmed our land about 2.1%, and the and ice sheets have absorbed the rest – – Arctic sea ice has absorbed 0.8%, the Greenland ice sheet has absorbed 0.9%, Antarctica about 0.2% and the rest by other glaciers. I wonder just how much more the ocean can handle and when the percentage of $CO_2$ will rise past that 2,1 level. Just look at the havoc that 2.1 level has had on droughts, floods, hurricanes and water evaporation."

## MORE HURRICANES AND RAIN

—"Why have we had increased rains, hurricanes and tornadoes?"

—"The ocean absorbs most of the heat from the global warming. This leads to increased evaporation of the water. The warmer air can hold more water vapor. But when the air cools at the higher altitudes it can't hold all the excess water. This gives us increased rain inland from the oceans. The northern plains area of the U.S.A. has had heavy rains from water that had been evaporated from the Pacific. And the inland countries of Europe get what was evaporated from the north Atlantic.

"The torrential summer rains have inundated central Europe and caused devastating floods. Prague, my favorite city, was partially under water. Floods are normally much more common in the winter from rain and snow melting. There is a great deal of speculation that the recent summer floods are caused by global warming.

"With warmer oceans the hurricanes get stronger. The average hurricane has winds 50% stronger today than they had 40 years ago and the number of the strongest hurricanes has doubled. A rise in the world's sea surface temperatures is the primary contributor to the formation of stronger hurricanes. Since 1970 the average temperature of the ocean has risen 0.5 degrees. In the Gulf of Mexico it has risen 3 degrees recently. In the 1970s, the average number of intense Category 4 and 5 hurricanes occurring globally was about 10 per year. Since then it has more than doubled. Category 4 hurricanes have sustained winds from 131 to 155 mph. Category 5 systems, such as Hurricane Katrina that destroyed New Orleans, had winds of 156 mph or more. Another recent hurricane set a record with winds at 175 mph."

—"How can we have more rain and more drought?"

—"While increased rain and storms will affect parts of the world, increased heat and dryness will affect other parts. Lands affected by drought have doubled since 1970.

"Southern Europe is predicted to warm considerably as the century stumbles along under the burden of global warming. While we saw temperatures rise significantly in the early years of this century, we also saw the water tables dropping as less rain cooled the summer swelter. Forest fires from Portugal to Greece warned us of the parching earth, which was becoming less friendly to the farmer.

"Is the Sahara leaping over the Mediterranean? The mounting evidence is that it is more than a momentary flight of the Fahrenheit—it is the result of the increased global warming. It is the desertification of the fertile lands that gave us the Renaissance, the Age of Discovery, the Age of Enlightenment, and the Industrial Revolution. By century's end Italy's average temperature is predicted to rise by 8 degrees—ten times the last century's temperature rise. The number of uncomfortably hot days of 35 degrees Celsius, 95 Fahrenheit, should increase tenfold. Rainfall is predicted to drop 15%. Farming will be decimated.

"Tourism will drop as people leave the beaches of Spain for those of Denmark and Norway. Emigration from southern Europe will increase and the northern EU countries will be the destinations.

"Portugal has experienced severe drought, their worst in history. Crops have died as have their farm animals. Another problem is that as the rivers carry less water, hydroelectric plants cannot put out the electricity of which they are capable.

"In China, sub-Saharan Africa, and Kazakhstan the deserts are expanding--sometimes because of poor farming methods and sometimes because of diverting the water upstream, which makes the downstream communities waterless. A related problem is that when lakes, rivers and seas dry up, the fish will die. The Aral Sea, which once supplied a million pounds of fish yearly, is now a dry hole. Lake Chad, in Africa, once the continent's largest body of water, has been reduced to 5% of its former girth. Diseases like malaria have increased in the higher altitudes, such as in Kenya, which used to be too cold for mosquitoes. There will be more pressure for North Africans to emigrate northward. It's not fair, but the countries that cause most of the global warming are not suffering from it as much as many of the Third World countries."

## COST OF GLOBAL WARMING TO BUSINESSES AND TO INDIVIDUALS

—"As a businessman, what might global warming cost my business?"

—"Insurance costs will go up. Damage costs from the three most expensive types of storms-- hurricanes in the United States, typhoons in Japan and rainstorms in Europe -- will nearly double if carbon dioxide emissions double their current rate. If we do nothing, increased hurricanes in the US will increase hurricane insurance to nearly double, to $150 billion. Japanese typhoon costs would nearly double to $34 billion. Flood insurance in Europe will rise significantly to about $150 billion. The consumer will pay the costs in increased prices. And taxes will increase for a number of expenses such as preventative measures, aid to victims, low interest loans and clean up.

"Global warming is affecting people's health in various ways as warming moves northward. Allergy seasons are lengthening, tropical diseases, like malaria and encephalitis, are moving northward. Fresh water systems from the Great Lakes to your local lake, to your local municipal water company are subject to an increase in algae, such as Cyanobacteria, that are linked to a number of diseases—from skin to nerves. Then with warmer temperatures people will need more water to prevent dehydration and kidney stones. Few people drink enough water anyway. Then we find that with more warm weather we are getting far more insects and insect bites and stings.

### IT IS AN UNSOLVABLE PROBLEM UNLESS WE TAKE DRASTIC ACTION

"So while the Earth has been able to handle the natural amounts of carbon in the oceans and on the land, we have added to the problem by going deep into the ground for more sources of carbon in coal, oil and gas –then burned them. We have gone far past what nature can handle. The carbon is here to stay. It is picked up by trees and other plants while they grow, then released when they die. It is picked up in the oceans in plankton and in shellfish then released when they die and decompose. So the carbon that has always been a part of the life of the Earth just re-circulating from air to water to plants to the soil – is never removed. But the carbon that has been in a long sleep, far below the Earth's surface, has been awakened and threatens us as a malevolent ghost of our evolutionary past. Even if we added more trees to the land and clams to the ocean, we won't be able to exorcise this carbonic ghost."

—"Maybe we can build a huge exhaust pipe into outer space and get rid of it that way. It's certainly not practical to send one or two thousand rocket ships full of carbon into space every day. We had better find a practical solution fast."

## SOLUTIONS

"If it's true, like Toynbee said, that 'civilizations don't have to die—because they are not organisms, but rather products of wills'—then we have a chance."

–"But the civilizations that he studied died, that was his life mission—to study 'why.'"

--"But no civilization of the past has faced the threat that our whole species faces today. Maybe a few can realize that many people are living beyond the means that the planet can support but can enough of the world's population see it, believe it, and start to do the drastic things needed to make it happen?"

—"Nature won't clear up the mess we have caused. We have to do it. We must find ways to reduce the greenhouse gases we produce and somehow store those we have produced."

—"I think you guys should do it. I still want my Humvee with its 6 miles to the gallon. I want speed and power. I want air conditioning in my twelve room house and in my car."

—"I know that you're saying that somewhat tongue in cheek but the realities are that people don't want to sacrifice. Just look at the American personal debt. The average American not only wants to have everything he or she already has, they want every one of the latest gadgets, cars, video games and home appliances that is advertised. And they want it now!"

—"Heck, they want the homes they can't afford—and the second home they can't afford. They want the boat they can't afford and the vacation they can't afford. There are so many living in a plastic card dream world—and it usually becomes a nightmare. Do you think that these people are willing to sacrifice anything? No matter how minor?"

—"It's a self centered morality that generally predominates over what's good for society or even what's good for themselves in the future. Eat, drink and be merry, for tomorrow we die—or go bankrupt. Look at the number of bankruptcies and home mortgage foreclosures of a few years ago. Home owners couldn't make their house payments. The mortgage lenders went bankrupt. The stock market

32

dropped. Everything financially is inter-related. Our planet is in a worse condition than the home mortgage lenders. But the world can't declare bankruptcy. Either we live or we die. We won't get a second chance like an over-mortgaged home owner.

"The Kyoto Protocol of 1997 was a major governmental step in recognizing and fighting global warming. A major problem was that the two biggest polluters, the U.S. and China, either refused to follow it or were exempted. But the U.S. has opened more factories and China has planted a lot of trees and coal burning power plants to feed the trees. I don't know why our country couldn't at least have gone on a tree planting binge."

—"Probably because trees don't produce oil—or maybe the major manufacturers can't make artificial trees that would undersell the nurseries."

—"Oh my! Do I detect a note of sarcasm, Ray?"

—"More than a note—a whole symphony of sarcasm. I've really been embarrassed by my country's stands on clean air, recycling, and conservation. When I visited the Vatican I saw that the Italians not only recycled their glass, but they had separate bins for clear, brown and green glass. And in Turkey you may find bins for glass, plastic, paper or metal.

"But there is another area to be considered. Some people want to boycott decorative woods like teak and mahogany that are used in fine furniture and as walls and other appointments in homes and offices. These woods have come from the trees of the rainforest that eat so much of the air's carbon. So that sounds like a noble gesture. But often they don't consider that the wood they burn in their fireplaces not only came from $CO_2$ breathing trees, but burning them released the carbon back into the air. So they decry the cutting of trees in which the carbon is preserved in the wood, but applaud the burning of other trees because it may save on electricity, which may have been produced by coal. We need much more comprehensive thinking about how to most effectively conserve! "

—"Before my trip, when I lived here at the lake, if I wanted to recycle I had to pay the trash company extra to take recyclables. At the same time my Norwegian mother-in-law had to sort her trash into three bins, one for paper, one for biodegradable garbage and one for plastics and other long lived materials. And this was in addition to her sorting out the glass and putting it in public bins and returning bottles and cans to the market to get her deposit back. And the deposit was substantial. A large Coke bottle brought 35 cents and a small bottle or can was 17 cents. The deposit made it financially worthwhile to bring them back. This along with the Norwegian concern for their beloved 'nature' made it mandatory. But also it was so easy to return the bottles and cans in a user friendly machine that took your bottles and gave you your automatic refund.

"But back to Kyoto. It was predicted that by 2080 there would be an 11% decrease in rainfall for farmland in developed countries due to climate change. And 65 developing countries might lose 280 million tons of cereal production. One of the objectives was to have developed countries buy carbon emission credits from countries that had more forests and plants. That money could then be used to help underdeveloped countries develop more effective agricultural techniques and to aid them in developing bioenergy. Bioenergy is a real alternative to fossil fuels and could include fuel from animal and plant waste and alcohol developed from plants. It was hoped that by using biofuels carbon emissions could be reduced by between 5 and 25 percent of projected fossil fuel emissions for the year 2050. But it has got to become more pollution free in its development.

"Then the protocol looked to developing carbon sinks, places where carbon could be stored—like forests. It also stated that the destruction of forests was responsible for a quarter of all greenhouse gases. By encouraging forest growth in undeveloped countries the polluting countries could buy credits from the people with the forests to offset the carbon they were releasing. So for example, if the U.S. was told that its carbon dioxide target was 4 billion tons by 2030 and it was putting out 5 billion tons, it could buy credits for the extra billion tons from countries with forests, like Brazil or some undeveloped country that had planted a lot of trees.

"The Montreal Protocol of 1987 on protecting the ozone layer and the Kyoto Protocol on climate change gave the less developed countries more time to follow the rules. China and India have taken advantage of this leniency by producing the highly damaging fluorocarbon HCFC for air conditioners for countries that still allow it. Europe banned them years ago. The U.S. followed slowly. But most countries still allow them so these refrigerants, which gram for gram are thousands of times more damaging than CO2, are increasing at about 50% a year. Not only that, but the Chinese are collecting millions of dollars from a United Nations agency for destroying a waste gas which is a byproduct of making the harmful refrigerant. And you thought the Chinese were just making money making shoes!

"The Chinese do make air conditioners for Europe with the safer, but more expensive, modern refrigerants. Many countries are pushing for a faster phase out of HCFC-22, but the Chinese are fighting it. It seems as though it is not only the Americans who are holding back on climate change technologies for the good of business."

—"Hold it Wreck, not all American companies are blind to ecological concerns. At least one company is making huge efforts to capture carbon dioxide from its coal burning electricity generating plants. Chilled ammonia is being used to trap CO2. This will use between 15 and 30% of the plant's output to accomplish. So more coal will have to be burned and consumers will have to pay more. But the world will profit. Other approaches are to liquefy the CO2 by cooling it, possibly by applying a half ton of pressure per square inch to the captured gas, then storing the liquefied gas thousands of feet below the earth's surface. Other plants are capturing the carbon dioxide and selling it to soft drink makers for carbonated beverages.

"The Germans are way ahead of us in developing non-polluting energy. There are so many options. We can generate power by using the motion of the ocean waves. Having machines that convert the mechanical energy of the up and down motion of the ocean waves into electrical energy is a huge potential energy source, as is wind, tidal power, solar power and a number of other energy sources that become more and more desirable as petroleum prices increase and the desirability of coal and nuclear power decrease. It's just a matter of priorities. And some people are beginning to put planetary survival higher on their list of 'must do' things. Too bad that for many people it still ranks behind playing video poker!

"People don't realize the environmental costs the energy they use. For example, to burn 100 W bulb for a year would use 714 pounds of coal or 143 pounds of natural gas or 32 hours of solar power from a hundred square meters of solar panels or 35 minutes of a 1.5 million watt turbine working at 100% efficiency.

"If every American would replace just one 100 W light bulb with an Energy Star bulb it would save enough energy to light 3 million homes for a year and would save nearly $700 million in annual energy bills. It would also reduce the greenhouse gas output by 4,500,000 tons-- about the equivalent of 800,000 cars. But we Americans are too self-centered, I'm afraid."

"Sad but true, Con. We Americans are so uninformed. Compared to other regions we are less informed about climate change and we are less likely to believe that we humans, especially we American, are responsible for it. One of my major goals is to make everyone aware of climate change. This should then focus on why we need to reduce population and finally how we can make our population better, more loving and less violent by making an effort to have capable loving adults having children,.

People need to know about the problem. Polls by various agencies in 2010 showed that about 25% of Europeans and Americans were not concerned with climate change—and the number of such people is increasing.  People nearly everywhere, including majorities in developed Asia and Latin America, are more likely to attribute global warming to human activities rather than to natural causes. The U.S. is the exception, with nearly half (47%) – and the largest percentage in the world – attributing global warming to natural causes."(7)

## NOTES

1. May 22, 2014 | Washington, DC - See more at:
http://www.thechicagocouncil.org/files/Global_Agricultural_Development_Initiative/files/Global_Agricultur e/Initiative_Events/Global_Food_Security_Symposium_2014.aspx#sthash.pZYUKM18.dpuf)

2. Journal of Global Biogeochemical Cycles, Feb. 14, 2008

3. U.S, New and World Report, July 10, 1967, p. 38: Saturday Review, Apr. 1, 1967, p. 52

4. State of the Climate in 2013 NOAA's National Climatic Data Center)

5. Rudolf Wu. Environmental Science and Technology. May 2006

6. Proceedings of the National Academy of Sciences, October 2007

7. Ray, Julie; Anita Pugliese (22 April 2011). "Worldwide, Blame for Climate Change Falls on Humans". Gallup.Com. Retrieved 3 May 2011.